Alan L. Berger

WITNESS TO THE SACRED

MYSTICAL TALES OF PRIMITIVE HASIDISM

NEW HORIZONS PRESS
Chico, CA
1977

Copyright © 1977 by Alan L. Berger

All rights Reserved, including all translation rights.

Acknowledgement: All illustrations are originals in this study and have been copyrighted separately by Ellen Steinfeld, 338 Scott Ave., Syracuse, .N.Y. 13224 No reproduction of any of these drawings may be done without the written consent of the artist.

Printed in the U.S.A.
NEW HORIZONS PRESS
P.O. BOX 1758
Chico, CA. 95927

LIBRARY OF CONGRESS
CATALOGING IN
PUBLICATION DATA

Berger, Alan L 1939-
   Witness to the sacred.

   Includes bibliographical references and index.
   1. Tales, Hasidic--History and criticism.
   2. Mysticism--Judaism. I. Title.
BM532.B46   296.7'1   77-11871
ISBN 0-914914-11-1
ISBN 0-914914-10-3 pbk.

To Nomi, Ariel and Michael
for their understanding,
wisdom and presence

CONTENTS

Introduction 7
Hasidic Tales: History and Theory 13
Text 23
Mysticism in the Tales 28
Modification of Traditional
  Interpretive Models 34
Analysis of Specific Tales 39
Conclusion 61
Index of Hasidic Terms 63

Illustrations

Five Hasidim 6
Elevating Divine Sparks 12
Devekuth, Kavvanah 15
Saying Torah 18
The Besht 22
Against the Evil Eye 25
Besht Receives Two Holy Letters 30
Worship in Corporeality 37
Swift Travel 40
Melamed's Dream Palace 52

Five Hasidim Dancing on Shin. The Hebrew Letter Shin is the First letter of the word Shaddai (Almighty).

Copyright © 1977 Ellen Steinfeld

Introduction

My intention is to present a perspective on mysticism which suggests a 'normalized' element. Specifically, I hope to demonstrate that normalized mysticism displays a shift in emphasis from theosophical concerns, i.e., information about "upper worlds," to the sociological or communal dimension, employing examples from eighteenth-century Hasidism. Hasidic *praxis* emphasized *'avodah be-gashmiyyut* (worship in corporeality). Transformation of ordinary and mundane activity illuminate religious behavior and experience. ". . . secular deeds such as eating, drinking, nonsense conversations, etc., . . . are ways of worshiping God, if only man will know . . . to accompany his physical deeds with spiritual *devekuth*" (adhesion to, or communion with God).[1] This study deals with one particular aspect of worship in corporeality, the telling of tales. It treats the specificity of tales concerning Israel ben Eliezer, the Baal Shem

---

[1] Joseph G. Weiss, "Reshith Zimihtah shel ha Derek ha Hasidith," *Zion* (Jerusalem: The Jewish Historical Society of Israel, 1951), Nos. 3-4, p. 97.

Tov [Besht], founder of the Hasidic movement, and their functions as portraying a normalized mysticism; why they were told, what perceptions of the cosmos they reveal, and the nature of their audience.

The term 'normal mysticism' is employed by Max Kadushin in describing the potential spiritual significance of the commonplace. Kadushin is concerned almost exclusively with rabbinic *praxis*. Nonetheless his description of normal mysticism has validity far beyond the early period of Judaism, as well as for the mystical systems of other religious traditions.

> Normal mysticism enables a person to make normal, commonplace, recurrent situations and events occasions for worship. The food he eats, the water he drinks, the dawn and the twilight are joined to berakot (blessings) acknowledging God's love, but they arouse in the individual, in the same act of worship, a poignant sense of the nearness of God.[2]

Two significant criteria of normal mysticism are "an awareness of God's nearness," and the telescoping of past and future events into "manifestations of God's love in the present."[3] The awareness of God's nearness is attested in such concepts as "prayer, repentance, Torah study," and other daily activities. Bizarre or unusual occurrences, including visions, are not necessary.[4] Rather, it is the daily and familiar things which

---

[2]Max Kadushin, *Worship and Ethics* (Evanston: Northwestern University Press, 1964), p. 168.

[3]*Ibid.*, p. 171.

[4]Kadushin does, however, make exception to his observation. He notes "There were some individuals ... whose valuational life was affected by abnormal psychologic states, such as visions and locutions, and rabbinic theology by no means excluded religious experience of that type. There was ... room for that experience of God which was a factor in an *abnormal* [my emphasis] state of the valuational life, in other words for *abnormal* [my emphasis] mysticism." *Organic Thinking* (New York: Bloch Publishing Co., 1938), p. 238.

stimulate the experience of God. Normal mysticism is paradoxical. It is comprised of both a noncommunicable factor — awareness of divine nearness, and a communicable and 'conceptualized' factor — consciousness of God's love and justice.[5] "*Middat rahamim* (God's Love), *middat ha-din* (God's justice) and *berakot* are," contends Kadushin, "elements in the common vocabulary."[6] Hence they are available to the ordinary man, as well as to the religious specialist.

Normalized mysticism is, I believe, a more accurate and less polemical term than normal mysticism. Kadushin, on his part, implies the same insidious and hierarchical varieties of mysticism as were displayed from the Catholic perspective in Robert Zaehner's *Mysticism Sacred and Profane* (New York: Oxford, 1957). My use of the term normalized mysticism is not concerned with evaluating, but rather with describing a religious structure, mysticism, which has undergone a particular process of change. It is not my intention to trace the genetic-historical development of Hasidism from its Kabbalistic (sixteenth-century) and Sabbatian (seventeenth-century) roots and heritage. I employ normalized mysticism as descriptive of the early Hasidic movement because Hasidism takes the normal, everyday institutions of mankind and works through them. Beshtian Hasidism utilized the ordinary and familiar as vehicles for divine worship. The 'world' was perceived as a vehicle to normalize mystical experience, making this experience a possibility for the masses, and not merely for the spiritual elite. In this sense, normal appears to be an appropriate term. Thus Kadushin, despite his choice of polemics, is helpful in pointing to the nature of mysticism in Beshtian Hasidism.

Normalized mysticism functions by taking seriously the social world. Historical events and human institutions become

---

[5]*Ibid.*, p. 181.

[6]*Ibid.*, p. 168.

legitimately associated with mysticism.[7] Normalization is anthropologically oriented; its effects are therefore pragmatic, manifested as a concern for daily conduct and activity. Ethical and moral behavior are emphasized. This stands in contrast to what might be termed elite or, as Max Weber would have it, "world-fleeing contemplation."[8] Here the effort tends to be contemplative rather than active, and is defined either in terms of transcending the 'world,' or by types of theosophical speculation. In brief, normalized mysticism functions by linking sacred elements of the cosmos with events in the secular realm. Normalized mysticism is identifiable by five major characteristics: 1) availability and transmission of the experience to all men regardless of their level of religious virtuosity, and including those who are, in Weber's terms, "religiously unmusical"; 2) a 'this-worldly' soteriology; 3) a strong communal association; 4) an 'enthusiastic' response; and 5) a pronounced emphasis upon the experiential element. A major contribution of normalization is its perception of mysticism as a structure

---

[7]A similar argument is advanced by Friedrich von Hügel. He contends that there is "no distinct, self-sufficing, purely mystical mode of apprehending reality." 'Wholesome' mysticism is concerned with the "concrete, contingent, historical institutional in thought and action." *The Mystical Element of Religion* (London: J.M. Dent, 1961), Vol. II, pp. 283 and 306.

[8]Weber's typology of mysticism included "world-fleeing contemplation," and inner-worldy mysticism. The former he describes as a "subjective condition of a distinctive kind, . . . confined to a minority who have particular religious qualifications, and (is) the end product of the systematic execution of . . . contemplation." Max Weber, *The Sociology of Religion,* translated by Ephraim Fischoff (Boston: Beacon Press, 1968), p. 168. Weber never systematically developed the "ideal type" of inner-worldly mysticism, although he correctly believed that this type of mysticism did not seek to "escape involvement in worldly status . . . ."

within the context of daily human religiosity.

Certain mystical movements have consciously attempted to 'normalize' the privileged religious experience of the founder, saints, or other exemplary figures in the tradition. Normalization has been noted with great clarity, for example, in the Islamic tradition by Gustave von Grunebaum.

> Once you recognize ecstasy as a legitimate form of religious life and once you admit that this aim should be open not only to an elite but to the masses, this attitude necessarily leads to forms of organized mysticism such as crystallized in Sufism. An ever larger number of the faithful can attain the ultimate experience of the divine union by participating in an association where such experience is facilitated by technical means, by a certain mode of life of the community or the order.[9]

Franciscan legends in the Christian tradition appear to point toward normalization as well. Hasidism, for its part, "represents an attempt to make the world of kabbalism, through a certain transformation or reinterpretation, accessible to the masses of the people, and . . . it was . . . extraordinarily successful."[10] Early Hasidic mysticism emphasizes the community. Societal phenomena are transformed into concerns of mysticism. This concern "is expressed in such doctrines as the worship of God through every material act" *('avodah be-gashmiyyut)*.[11] The mechanism of normalized mysticism in the Hasidic tradition is suggested by M. Buber's observation that "in Hasidism . . . mysticism has become ethos."[12]

---

[9]Cited by Gershom Scholem in "Mysticism and Society," *Diogenes* (Montreal: American Academy of Arts and Sciences, 1967), p. 16.

[10]Gershom G. Scholem, *Major Trends in Jewish Mysticism* (New York: Schocken, 1969), pp. 327-328. Hereafter this will be cited as *Major Trends*.

[11]Rivkah Schatz-Uffenheimer, "Hasidism," *Encyclopaedia Judaica* (Jerusalem: Keter, 1972), p. 1408.

[12]Martin Buber, *The Origin and Meaning of Hasidism*, trans. M. Friedman (New York: Horizon Press, 1960), pp. 198-99.

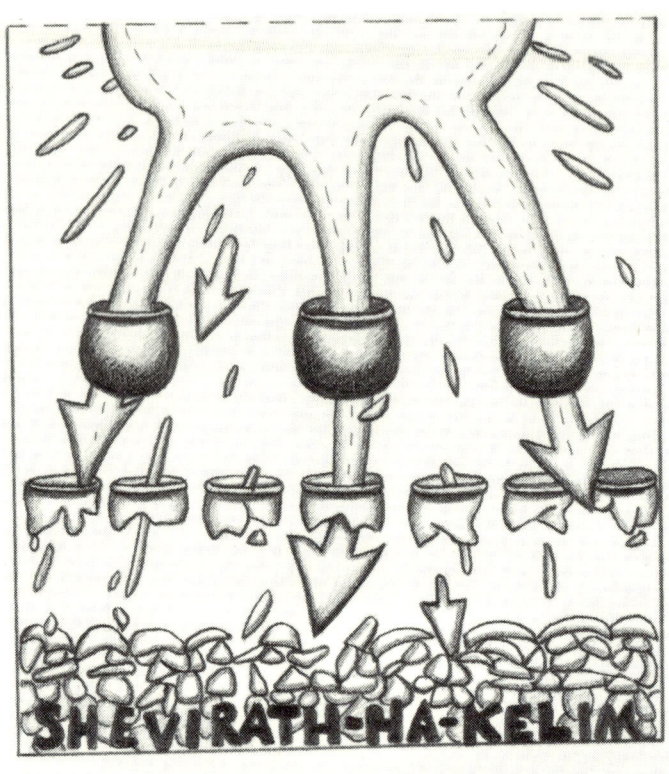

Elevating Divine Sparks
Copyright © 1977 Ellen Steinfeld

Hasidic Tales: History and Theory

Specifically, Hasidic *praxis* reflects a concretization of the cosmogony of the sixteenth-century kabbalist Isaac Luria. Luria's theory, as mediated through the works of his disciple Hayim Vital, stressed the necessity of "raising the [divine] sparks" *('aliyath ha-nitsotsoth)*. These sparks had become imprisoned in matter owing to a primal 'accident' — the "breaking of the vessels" *(shevirath ha-kelim)* designed to hold them. Man's "intention" or "meditation" *(kavvanah)* in prayer, attests Luria, can assist the sparks, which are covered by "shells" *(kelipoth)* of matter, to ascend. The process of "restoration" *(tikkun)* of harmony — both in the upper worlds and on earth — is then completed. Beshtian Hasidism overlooked the kabbalistic distinction between divine and human sparks, and normalized the doctrine of *'aliyath ha-nitsotsoth*. This process has been noted succinctly by B. Weinryb.

> "Uplifting of the sparks" of divine life... in Hasidism came to mean (among other things) that since holy sparks were supposed to be everywhere there is no sphere of life devoid of significance. This

transformed profane things into holy ones, and endowed material matters with religious value. In Hasidism . . . the emphasis shifted from the catastrophic origin and the "other side" (evil) to the existence of sparks of divine light everywhere, inevitably endowing all activity with an essential spark of divinity.[13]

Hasidic expression reflects a new conception of what is the center of the religious life of its adherents. Activity in the "upper worlds" remains important, but primarily because of its ramifications in daily communal life. Mystical activity is no longer restricted to the isolated 'specialist.' "Of the exalted kabbalistic cosmology that had been limited to a few chosen spirits, Hasidism," observes S. Spiegel, "made a religious folk-movement, a reality of community life."[14]

Hasidic tales[15] illustrate the possibility of raising sparks even while engaged in *'avodah be-gashmiyyut*. Three separate yet closely related techniques help one achieve this goal: 1) *devekuth*

[13]Bernard D. Weinryb, *The Jews of Poland* (Philadelphia: The Jewish Publication Society, 1973), p. 271.

[14]Shalom Spiegel, *Hebrew Reborn* (New York: Macmillan, 1930), p. 150.

[15]The role of the tale in Judaism dates to the Old Testament. There the term *mashal,* often in association with *hidah* (riddle) referred to similitude, parable, example story and other genre types. Richard Dorson has noted "among the Jewish people the telling of stories and the learning of the faith are interwoven in a manner unparalleled in other countries of Western civilization." Tales in the medieval period, however, were for the use of women and children. Collections such as the *Ma'aseh Book* were considered religiously inferior. Hasidic *praxis* departed from this view, incorporating the tale into religious ritual for men. The *zaddik's* ability to tell tales elevated them to the level of "recited Torah." This resulted in an oral tradition which greatly appealed to the untutored. Tales were incorporated into a distinct literary genre, i.e., "literature of praise." Storytelling became not only a way of communicating Hasidic mystical *praxis* and beliefs on a popular level, but also a ritual for participating in mystical experience.

Devekuth, Kavvanah

Copyright © 1977 Ellen Steinfeld

during everyday occupations, 2) *kavvanah* — correct intention or meditation, and 3) by telling and listening to tales praising the *zaddikim* (Hasidic holy men). There is an intimate relationship between these activities. Worship in corporeality symbolizes Hasidism's communal interest. The microcosmic-macrocosmic analogy implicit in mystical *praxis*[16] becomes, in Hasidism, more concrete and ordinary, its effects are experienced in the daily and familiar activity of community members. All tales as well as the deeds of the *zaddik* portrayed therein are valuable in helping to raise imprisoned divine sparks.

The Hasidic tale is properly understood as a *hieros logos*, a sacred story. It functions by proclaiming "some definite occurrence," and "it determines the hearer's salvation."[17] The tales are "revelatory" in the sense of raising divine sparks, thereby stimulating salvific action. Von der Leeuw, although specifying the *hieros logos* in Christianity, suggests that the association of the story and proclamation of salvation may rightly be called the "Word of God."[18] This "Word" implies both announcement and actually-present divine power and is the form of revelation in general. Hence, the telling of a tale represents a form of religious behavior. Questions can be asked concerning the tales' effect on the hearer as well as the setting in which they are told. But the content of the tale is no less "revelatory" than

---

[16]The *Tiqqune Ha-Zohar* (130b), for example, reports that "The limbs of man are all arranged in the order of the beginning ('al sidrē bĕrēshīt) — i.e., of the mystical days of creation which are identical with the six lower sefirot — " and man is therefore called a microcosm ('olam qatan)." Cited by A. Altmann, "The Delphic Maxim in Medieval Islam and Judaism," in *Biblical and Other Studies*, ed., A. Altmann (Cambridge: Harvard University Press, 1963), p. 208.

[17]Gerardus Von der Leeuw, *Religion in Essence and Manifestation*, trans. J. Turner (New York: Harper & Row, 1963), Vol. II, p. 418.

[18]*Ibid.*, p. 420.

narration itself. Various ways of worship and religious behaviors are indicated. The ideal of spirituality shifts from vigorous ascetic practices. Excessive fasting, prolonged prayer, and detailed Talmudic exegesis *(pilpul)* are no longer primary values. In their place are basic Jewish ethical and moral maxims, e.g., charity, mercy, piety and devotion presented as the socioreligious norm. An elite, rabbinic value — erudition in Torah study is replaced by a 'folk' or popular element, the behavior of the *zaddik* — compassion, enthusiasm, and the ability to achieve *devekuth*. The ideal type of holy man shifts from the scholar *(talmid hakham)* to the *zaddik*, who has become Torah. The *zaddik* is the center of the tales. He reveals and personifies a particular ethical virtue. The mystical element is implicit in the *zaddik's* ability to sustain the religious well-being of his followers. The *zaddik's* role is both "cosmic," i.e., mediating between upper and lower worlds, and social — helping those on the margins of society in their quest for salvation and comfort.[19] The holy man, by concretizing the possibility of *devekuth,* effectively normalized mysticism.

Tales were employed on ritual occasions such as the *se'udah shelishith* (third sabbath meal). Here the table of the *zaddik* is an "altar of God."[20] The "meal" was a social institution at which

---

[19]Subsequent *zaddikim* appear to have emphasized either the cosmic or the social aspect of mystical leadership. For example, the nineteenth century *dissident* Hasidism of both Przysucha and Kotzk warned against the decadence, i.e., 'trivialization' of Hasidism. The needs of the common people *viz.,* the social dimension of *zaddikism,* were viewed as a waste of the *zaddik's* time and talent. For an interesting discussion of this phenomenon see Abraham J. Heschel's *A Passion for Truth* (New York: Farrar, Straus & Giroux, 1973), which compares Menahem Mendle of Kotzk and Søren Kierkegaard. On the general question of the "seclusion" *(hitboddut)* of the *zaddik*, see Samuel H. Dresner's suggestions in *The Zaddik* (London, New York, Toronto: Abelard-Schuman, 1960), p. 269.

[20]Samuel Horodezky, *Leaders of Hasidism,* trans. A. Magasanik (London: Hasefer, 1932), p. 131.

Saying Torah at the Third Sabbath Meal

Copyright © 1977 Ellen Steinfeld

time mystical activity by the *zaddik* was expected.[21] Hasidim remained far into the night "to listen to the living words of God," spoken by the *zaddik*. The numinous aspect of the occasion — semi-darkness, close contact with the holy man — is underscored by the fact that those attempting to abruptly halt the proceeding suffer either excommunication and death, or grave consequences are foretold for the entire town in which the disturbance occurred.[22] But storytelling was not restricted to any particular time. Telling stories of the miraculous deeds of the *zaddikim* became a

[21]Hasidim celebrated four meals on the sabbath: *se'udah rishonah (se'udah Abraham Avinu)*, celebrated on Friday night; *se'udah shenith (se'udah Yitzhok Avinu)*, served at noon on Saturday; *se'udah shelishith (se'udah Yaakob Avinu)*, which begins at sundown on Saturday; and *se'udah David Ha-Melekh*, also called *melaveh malkah*, held late Saturday night. Here "no Torah is said by the Rebbe, instead the time is spent in merriment, consisting of singing and dancing." Jacob S. Minkin, *The Romance of Hasidism* (North Hollywood: Wilshire Book Company, 1971), p. 330.

The third meal, traditionally, was the time when the *zaddik* provided a mystical exegesis. Certan scholars have undervalued the numinous character of "saying Torah" at the third meal. "The more profound and mysterious the *zaddik's* sermon is, the more holy it is for the listener. The less they (the Hasidim) understand the words, the more respect and reverence they hold it in." Torsten Ysander, *Studien zum B'estschen Hasidismus* (Uppsala Universitets: Arsskrift, 1933), p. 320. The *melaveh malkah* was typically the time when tales were related. However, the collection of tales upon which this study is based departs from this practice; the *se'udah shelishith* is the occasion for both exegesis and tales.

The *se'udah shelishith* was "the weekly highlight of communal religiosity focused on social intercourse." Weiss, "A Circle of Pneumatics in Pre-Hasidism," *Journal of Jewish Studies* (London: Jewish Chronicle Publications, 1957), Vol. VIII, p. 206.

[22]See tales 209 and 45 in Dan Ben-Amos, and Jerome R. Mintz (trans. and eds.), *In Praise of the Ba'al Shem Tov* (Bloomington/London: Indiana University Press, 1970). Hereafter this work will be cited *In Praise*. The tales are neither numbered nor titled in the various Hebrew editions.

"new religious value," and further, "there is something of the celebration of a religious rite about it."[23] To tell a tale is the equivalent of action. Tales not only extol the zaddikim, but are a ritual for summoning power. One can, for example, pray for a sick person with a tale, or save a drowning person with words.[24] On the one hand, the tales are pious homilies attesting to various miraculous occurrences. Yet, on the other hand, Hasidic tales achieved the "prestige" of theoretical discourse.

> The revival of a new mythology in the world of Hasidism . . . draws not the least part of its strength from its connection between the magical and the mystical faculties of its heroes. When all is said and done it is this myth which represents the greatest creative expression of Hasidism. In the place of the theoretical disquisition, or at least side by side with it, you get the Hasidic tale.[25]

The tales then are similar to 'performative utterances.' One does something in the act of telling the tale.

In sum, a major innovation of Hasidism is the utilization of tales as well as prayers for mystical purposes.[26] The implications for normalized mystical experience are recognized by the Hasidic tradition itself. The following tale is explicit on this matter.

> The Besht was narrating folk-stories to his disciples. Noting their surprise he told them the following parable: A king sent his son to take charge of a fortress situated near the frontier. He informed him that the enemy was planning an attack in the near future, and instructed him to store within the fortress all food procurable. If

---

[23]*Major Trends,* p. 349.

[24]See tales 114 and 220 *In Praise.*

[25]*Major Trends,* p. 349.

[26]*In Praise,* p. 337.

he could not secure food of superior quality, he was to fill every storehouse with food of poor grade. Though the king's counsel did not seem necessary to him, the prince obeyed. The siege of the fort continued a long time, and the coarse food in the end proved the safeguard against surrender. Likewise, my friends, store in your memory these common tales I narrate to you, as well as the teachings which seem to you profound. In your work among the people everything will prove useful.[27]

I cited the tale in full because it represents, in my opinion, three major features of normalization displayed in early Hasidic mysticism: 1) it illustrates the power of even 'common' tales to transmit mystical teachings, 2) the 'audience' to be reached is not restricted to the *virtuosi*, or immediate disciples, but includes the broadest possible spectrum of Jews, and 3) the salvation of the "fortress," i.e., Judaism, is to be founded upon the inclusion of the ordinary folk. The tale is distinguished from earlier, rabbinic material in its 'intention,' i.e., it is for everyone, and in its task, elevating fallen sparks. More importantly, unlike the rabbinic tale it is not primarily exegetical in the sense of explaining scriptural difficulties. The 'hero' of the tale is now the *zaddik*.

---

[27]Cited by Louis Newman (ed.), *The Hasidic Anthology* (New York: Schocken, 1968), p. 345.

The Besht

Copyright © 1977 Ellen Steinfeld

Text

More concretely, my analysis focuses upon normalized mystical experience as it is reflected in the Hasidic text *Shivhei ha-Besht*. The book was published in 1815 in Kopst (Poland), and six months later in Berdichev. It is the earliest published collection of Hasidic 'holy tales,' comprising a hagiographical account of the founder and first *zaddik* of Hasidism, Israel Baal Shem Tov (Besht).[28] This legendary "biography", although appearing fifty-five years after the founder's death, represents a *type of understanding* of the Hasidic holy man in connection with the daily problems and concerns experienced by his community. It remains a primary source of Hasidic "devotional" literature. The hagiographer's task, according to Hippolyte Delehaye, is not only to interest his audience, but primarily to edify them, "to do

---

[28] Numerous editions in both Hebrew and Yiddish have appeared since 1815, none of which number or titile the tales. I utilize the numbers and titles employed by the scholarly English translation, *In Praise* which is based upon the Kepst printing.

them good."[29] Reading, telling, and listening to the tales becomes a communal religious act. The writer of the book, Rabbi Dov Ber ben Samuel, denies having written either straightforward history or mere stories. His intention was rather to provide edifying recollections. This occurs on different levels, according to one's capacity — "The small and the great will find what fits them."[30] I am not claiming that any single text represents the essence of Hasidic mysticism.[31] However, the two-hundred and fifty-one tales in the Kopst edition are valuable for exploring the context of Hasidic religiomystical *praxis*.

The Besht is clearly identified with the lower strata of society. To his followers he was "not a man who established a theory or set forth a system; he himself was the incarnation of a theory and his whole life the revelation of a system."[32] Even the patently legendary elements in the tales are useful. They indicate the ideals and aspirations of Beshtian Hasidism. The Besht, for example, is reported as saying, "When one tells stories in praise of the *zaddikim*, it is though he were engaged in *Ma'aseh Merkavah*" (work of the chariot).[33] Consequently, relating deeds of the saints "was just as productive on the spiritual level as was the study of divine mysteries."[34]

---

[29]H. Delehaye, *The Legends of the Saints* (New York: Fordham University Press, 1962), p. 54.

[30]*In Praise*, p. 5.

[31]There are over three thousand extant Hasidic texts.

[32]Solomon Schechter, "The Chassidim," *Studies in Judaism* (New York: Dutton, 1958), p. 153.

[33]Reported *of* the Besht in the printer's preface, p.i. Reported *by* the Besht, p. 199. *In Praise*.

[34]Gershom G. Scholem, "Martin Buber's Interpretation of Hasidism," *The Messianic Idea in Judaism* (New York: Schocken, 1971), p. 233.

Against the Evil Eye

Copyright © 1977 Ellen Steinfeld

Tales in the *Shivhei ha-Besht* have two foci: on the one hand, they are the deeds of the holy man or *zaddik*, and on the other hand his community, the Hasidim.[35] The popular element of the tales is concerned with the welfare and religious virtue of the common Jew. The level of the supra-natural focuses upon the *praxis* of the *zaddik* in sustaining the religious well-being of his community. This activity includes ascents to the Messiah's "upper palace," visions, dream interpretations, and a variety of apotropaic activities including the writing and selling of amulets. The Besht possesses a special type of "marvelous" knowledge *(y'diah nifla'ah)*. This knowledge is superior to that of halakhic and kabbalistic scholars. It enables the holy man to repent sinners — one of his most important tasks, and to otherwise assist the members of his community. Marvelous knowledge permits the Besht to see into the minds and hearts of men, to know future events and to interpret what occurs in the upper worlds.

Hasidism had a special conception of the tale. Tales provided a means for traversing the gap between an "extra-ordinary norm" — the Lurianic notion of who was eligible to participate in what it perceived as an essentially meditative task, i.e., *'aliyath ha-nitsotsoth*, and what has become in Hasidic praxis a potentially "ordinary norm."[36] The setting of each tale follows a distinctive

---

[35]Buber has noted three circles which form around the mystic and are influenced by him: 1) the many who come to him from a distance, 2) those living in his neighborhood, and 3) his immediate disciples — the narrowest circle. *The Origin and Meaning of Hasidism*, ed. and trans. by Maurice Friedman (New York: Harper Torchbooks, 1960), pp. 141-45.

My use of mystical community encompasses all three of these circles. It refers to those who gather around or are influenced by the mystic, acknowledging him as a spiritual leader. It does not imply a community of mystics (specialists).

[36]Franklin Edgerton employs the terms "extraordinary" and "ordinary" norm in discussing two accepted, yet apparently opposed norms of human religious life in early India. "Dominant Ideas in the Formation of Indian Culture," *Journal of the American Oriental Society*

structure. The tale begins with the name of the informant, if known, "I heard from . . .," gives his occupation, and the geographical location. The setting is followed by the theme of the tale. The socioreligious implications connected with this type of communication have been noted by M. Eliade. He writes: "Privileged religious experiences, when they are communicated through a sufficiently impressive and fanciful scenario, succeed in imposing models or sources of inspiration to the whole community."[37]

(New Haven: American Oriental Society, 1942), p. 151.

[37]Mircea Eliade, *Myth and Reality,* trans. W. Trask (New York: Harper & Row, 1963), p. 147.

Mysticism in the Tales

Mircea Eliade, in his article "The Yearning for Paradise in Primitive Tradition," contends that mysticism, wherever it appears, whether in the ecstasy of the primitive shaman or in the "most recent and elaborate mysticism in existence," exhibits a yearning for paradise.[38] Eliade specifies characteristics of man in the 'paradisial' period. Focusing on those relevant to the Besht, one notes the following: ability to ascend to heaven, 'easy' access to the gods, friendship with animals and knowledge of their language, spontaneity, liberty, and immortality.[39] Eliade sounds a caveat, however, which bears repetition. "Both the Christian Saint and the shaman in ecstasy," he notes, "recover Paradise only provisionally; for neither — can abolish death — neither — can re-establish the condition of primordial man."[40] In my opinion, the activities of the Besht are clearly mystical.

---

[38]Eliade, "The Yearning for Paradise in Primitive Tradition," *Daedalus* (Cambridge: American Academy of Arts and Sciences, 1959), Spring, p. 261.

[39]*Ibid.*, p. 256.   [40]*Ibid.*, p. 263.

I treat now three of Eliade's characteristics: ascension, 'easy' access to the gods, and friendship with animals. All mysticism is, for Eliade, concerned with ascension symbolism, whether it be actual flight, levitation, climbing a ladder, or shamanic ascent to the sky.[41] He writes, "Whatever the content and value ascribed to ascensional experience — there remain always — two essential motifs — transcendence and freedom."[42] The *shivhei ha Besht* reports various ascents made by the Besht. He ascends in order to converse with the Messiah:

> With a great outcry I went to the palace of the Messiah. When our righteous Messiah saw me from afar he said to me, "Don't shout." He gave me two holy letters of the alphabet.[43]

Moreover, God is portrayed as being unable to resist the Besht's holiness.

> ... the Messiah said to the Besht, "I do not know whether you will open the gate, but if you do redemption will certainly come to Israel." He said that he heard God's voice saying to him: "What can I do with you since I must fulfill your will?"[44]

---

[41]Relevant here are the following of Mircea Eliade's works: *Myths, Dreams, and Mysteries,* trans. by P. Mairet (New York: Harper Torchbooks, 1960), pp. 99-122; *Patterns in Comparative Religion,* trans. by Rosemary Sheed (Cleveland and New York: The World Publishing Company, 1965), pp. 102-111; *Shamanism,* trans. by Willard R. Trask (New York: Pantheon Books, Bollingen Series LXXVI, 1963), pp. 122-44, 153-55, 165-67, 259-87 *passim;* and "The Yearning for Paradise in Primitive Tradition," pp. 255-67.

[42]Eliade, *Myths, Dreams, and Mysteries,* p. 108.

[43]*In Praise,* tale 41, p. 57.

[44]*Ibid.,* tale 42, p. 58.

The Besht Receives Two Holy Letters

Copyright © 1977 Ellen Steinfeld

Mysticism in the Tales

The Besht also ascends in order to discover proper halakhic answers to certain difficult exegetical problems whose solutions are inaccessible to earthly scholars.

> When the Besht's soul ascended (on Sabbath Eve during the Minhah prayer) to the palace of the *tosaphists* (twelfth to fourteenth century commentators on the Talmud) he did not find any improoo sion of the sin... Then he ascended (still higher) up to the *Rambam's* (Maimonides, died 1204) palace.... The (Besht) argued with the *Rambam*.... Then the *Rambam* conceded to (the Besht).[45]

Furthermore, the Besht is invisible.

> (The nobleman) said: "I did not see him." He said, "Since (the Besht) is a man who is able to make himself invisible at will, I will have to become reconciled with him."[46]

Ba'al Shem Tov is, in addition, a master of swift travel *(qfizat ha derek)*.[47] Flight, no matter what form it takes, signifies, according to Eliade, "intelligence, the understanding of secret things and metaphysical truths."[48]

Ba'al Shem Tov knows the language of animals. A disciple, Aryeh Leib of Polonnoye, wanted to learn "the language of the animals, birds, and palm trees," and he joined the Besht in order to fulfill this wish.[49]

---

[45] *Ibid.*, tale 227, pp. 232-33.

[46] *Ibid.*, tale 180, p. 193. Invisibility here saves the Besht's life, as the nobleman had sworn to kill him.

[47] See below the analysis of tale 238, "The Loose Woman" (pp. 19, 20 and 22).

[48] Eliade, *Myths, Dreams, and Mysteries,* p. 105.

[49] *In Praise,* tale 237, pp. 242-43.

The Besht said to him: "It is known to me that the main reason that you joined my group is to learn the language of birds and so on. Come here and I will explain it to you carefully."[50]

In the course of the Besht's explanation he articulates the microcosm-macrocosm relationship which was crucial in Beshtian Hasidic mysticism.

... the language of each animal in the upper chariot descends to the lower animals, beasts, and birds. The wise man who can understand and examine everything in its upper source in the upper chariot will be able to comprehend the origin of all the details and the means of the speech of the animals, beasts, and birds. This is the picture in general.

When he explained these things in detail, he revealed to (the disciple) awesome and wonderful secrets until he knew the matter thoroughly.

Then the Besht passed his hands over the (disciple's) face, and he forgot all the secret details of this knowledge.[51]

This tale is significant because it distinguishes between the specialist (mystic) and his disciples. While it appears that only the expert knows the hidden meanings of the universe, all are expected to worship God at their own level. It is not necessary to be a virtuoso in order to perceive the nearness of the divine.

Said the Besht: "Some seek God as if He were far removed from us and surrounded by many walls. They say (Song of Songs 3:1) 'I sought Him, but I found Him not.' Had they been wise, however, they would have known that 'no space is free of Him.' They can find Him in everything and everywhere, and they should understand

---

[50] *Ibid.*, p. 243.

[51] *Ibid.*, p. 244.

that 'one who attaches himself to any part of God is as if he were attached to the ALL in ALL."[52]

What the *zaddik* does or attains cannot be precisely replicated. He after all is a *zaddik*. The tension between the specialist and his community is, however, a creative one.[53] Hasidim are assisted by their *zaddik* in achieving the maximum of their potential for worship. Moreover, the entire thrust of the tales is in the direction of elevating the so-called common man.

---

[52] Cited by Newman, *op. cit., p. 156.*

[53] The mystic is defined by the intensity of his experience. Eliade, for example, observes that mystics "Live the sacred side of life in a profounder and more personal manner than other people." Eliade, *Myths, Dreams, and Mysteries.* The mystic is, therefore, a specialist in achieving an intense personal experience of the divine.
Concerning the tension between mystic and community in early Hasidism, Scholem observes:

> The fact is that from the beginning the Baal Shem — and his followers — were anxious to remain in touch with the life of the community; and to this contact they assigned an especial value.... Hasidism in fact solved the problem, at least as far as Judaism was concerned, of establishing so close a relation between the pneumatic (the mystic) — and the religious community — that the inevitable tension between them helps to enrich the religious life of the community instead of destroying it.

Major Trends, pp. 346-47.

Modification of Traditional Interpretive Models - Analogy with Jesus' Parables

In analyzing the specificity of the Hasidic tale, scholars of religion can benefit from the model of interpretive analysis of Jesus' parables suggested by Dan O. Via *(The Parables,* Philadelphia: Fortress Press, 1967). Hasidic tales are narrative legends. The hero's power is superior in *degree* to other men and to his environment. Although he is identified as a human being, the hero operates "in a world in which ordinary laws of nature are slightly suspended, . . . talking animals, . . . and talismans of miraculous power violate no rule of probability . . ."[54] The normalized element in mysticism can be made manifest by applying a variant of Via's exegesis of Jesus' parables. Parable is narrative giving as its picture "some interesting particular situation."[55] Parables are susceptible to a religio-literary

[54]Northrop Frye, *Anatomy of Criticism* (Princeton: Princeton University Press, 1957), p. 33.

[55]Rudolf Bultmann, *The History of the Synoptic Tradition,* trans. by J. Marsh (New York and Evanston: Harper & Row, 1963), p. 174.

analysis. They have a 'translatable content.' Via employs both a literary-analytical and existential-theological analysis of the parables, treating the narrative itself as crucial. The innerconnection of elements in the literary structure have meaning of their own as well as meaning in reference to historico-socioreligious occurrences. A text should be taken on its own terms. Parabolic significance is not primarily restricted, as Joachim Jeremias suggests, to information about Jesus' situation *(Sitz-im-Leben)*. On the contrary, meaning resides in *an understanding of the possibilities of existence* which his situation brought.[56]

The comparison between Jesus' parables and the tales of the Besht is justifiable on literary grounds. Both tell a similar story, but both also possess a variety of interpretations. Parable and tale are genres which self-consciously attempt to deal with the problem of the coalescing of divine presence and everyday life, i.e., normalized religious experience. Via addresses the specificity of the parable, but his observation is also valid for the Hasidic tale; "God and the world come together" showing life in the world to be meaningful.[57] Quite apart from the uniquely Christian concern for 'realized eschatology,' it is possible to observe a parallel function in the interpretive task for both parable and tale: "The event might occur once more in the exposition."[58] Language itself is capable of becoming an event. The hearer is involved in the subject matter.[59] The tales provide evidence of a distinct type of relationship between the holy man and his community. Hasidic tales (with Jeremias) furnish information concerning the uniqueness of the Besht, as well as affording knowledge about the *Sitz-im-Leben* of early Hasidism.

The Besht's tales, like Jesus' parables, are each composed of one of the two basic plot structures in Western literature, "comic" and

---

[56]Dan O. Via, Jr., *The Parables* (Philadelphia: Fortress Press, 1967), p. 39.

[57]*Ibid.*, p. 104.   [58]*Ibid.*, p. 52.   [59]*Ibid.*, p. 53.

"tragic." Comedy, in its broadest outline, means an ascent toward safety and the integration of the protagonist in a new or renewed community. Tragedy implies catastrophe and societal exclusion.[60] Characters in Jesus' parables are of the low mimetic, or realistic mode.[61] They are, in short, like us. The Hasidim share this trait with the parabolic actors. Where the tales differ from the Christian parables is in focally pointing toward the *zaddik* as instrumental in bringing about either integration or exclusion of the various actors.[62] Nonetheless, a literary analysis of Hasidic tales is justified on didactic grounds. For example, peculiarity of form and requisite type of analysis are shared by parable and tale.

> It is because the expression of thought is a subsidiary level in a parable, because ideas are found only implicity in the configuration of events, images, and encounters, that the parables, on the one hand, need interpretive clarification and, on the other, resist complete translation into any other terms.[63]

The literary form of the tale affords information about Hasidic doctrine by expressing the theoretical in pragmatic, concrete situations. The tales reflect actual problems which the Hasidic community faced, e.g., conversion, intermarriage, preoccupation with the self, etc. Tales attempted to organize the world such that these problems could be avoided and the community strengthened. The philosophical 'archetypes': *'avodah be-*

---

[60] Frye, *op. cit.*, p. 162.   [61] Via, *op. cit.*, p. 98.

[62] It should be noted that parable is a semitic story form. It has both Jewish and Christian permutations. (Bultmann, *op. cit.*, pp. 174ff.) Viewed from this perspective, Jesus' parables are but one type of parable. The Hasidic material may be seen as a late semitic variation.

[63] *Ibid.*, p. 32. Via's analysis falls into three categories: historico-literary criticism, literary-existential analysis, and existential-theological interpretation.

Worship in Corporeality

Copyright © 1977 Ellen Steinfeld

gashmiyyut, devekuth, kavvanah, and telling stories of the *zaddikim* are not ignored, but are presented in the tales within an experiential and empirical context. This type of analysis represents, in my opinion, a refining of the work of Joseph Dan and Martin Buber — two scholars who have devoted much attention to the Hasidic tale. Dan, in his book *Ha Novellah haHasidit (The Hasidic Novella),* has correctly stressed that the Hasidic tale is not a didactic story. It does not teach theory, nor can one employ the tale in order to understand *Hasidut.*[64] Dan is correct in so far as he goes. But, as we suggested above (p. 17), tales do in fact offer a form of instruction. Martin Buber, on the other hand, continually asserted the centrality of the legendary tale. It stood, for Buber, at the center of Hasidism's "religious-historical" development.[65] He compared Hasidic tales to the Zen *Koan,* for which he has been rightly criticized, and to Sufi literature.[66] But despite Buber's lifelong work with this genre, he never satisfactorily analyzed the mechanism by which the tales functioned. His presentation always was more homiletic than analytical.

---

[64]Joseph Dan, *Ha Novellah ha Hasidit* (Jerusalem: Bialik, 1966), p. 17.

[65]Martin Buber, "Interpreting Hasidism," *Commentary* (New York: The American Jewish Committee, 1963), p. 219.

[66]Scholem, "Martin Buber's Interpretation of Hasidism," pp. 249-50, and R.J. Zwi Werblowsky, "Some Observations on Recent Studies of Zen," *Studies in Mysticism and Religion,* ed. by Ephraim Urbach, *et al.* (Jerusalem: Magnes Press, 1967), p. 328. Buber makes his most explicit comparative statements on genre types in "Interpreting Hasidism." Also relevant here is his essay, "The Place of Hasidism in the History of Religion." *The Origin and Meaning of Hasidism,* pp. 220-39.

Analysis of Specific Tales

The first tale I have chosen to analyze is tale number 238, "The Loose Woman." It is valuable in illustrating how Via's model may be applied to Hasidic material.

> Once the rabbi, The Besht, was sitting at the third meal, and he was deep in thought. He did not say torah at the third meal at all which was unusual to the disciples. At the conclusion of that Sabbath he... had the wagon and horses prepared to travel, and he said that a few of the disciples would accompany him. He did not say where he was going. After they passed through the city gate, he ordered the disciples to turn their faces toward him, and he told the coachman as well to turn his face toward him and to tie the reins and let the horses go by themselves. By swift travel they covered a very long distance that night. They came to a big city, and the horses stopped at a large, ornate house.
>
> The Besht got down from his wagon. He took his pipe and went into the kitchen for a burning coal to light his pipe. As he entered, a young woman who had just gotten out of her bed also came into the

Swift Travel

Copyright © 1977 Ellen Steinfeld

kitchen half dressed. The Besht asked her to take a burning coal and put it in his pipe, and she did so. The Besht said to her: "Do you recognize me?"

She said: "No."

He said: "I am your uncle from Medzhibozh. What are you doing here?"

The woman said: "I was the householder's son's wife. My husband died and my father-in-law wants me to marry his nephew who is still a boy. I cannot oppose him, but it is against my will."

The Besht said to her: "Do not worry. I will be as a father to you, and if it is your desire, you can accompany me to my place today. There I will give you a good man that you will like for a husband."

The woman took her clothes and jewelry and put them in a box. When her father-in-law saw her doing this, he asked her: "Why are you preparing yourself? Where are you going?" She said to him: "This man is my uncle, and he wants to take me to his state where he will give me a husband."

The householder became angry at the Besht. He ran toward him furiously and said to him: "What are you doing to me, taking my daughter-in-law and all her clothing and jewelry without my knowledge?"

The Besht took him into a closed room and said to him: "Know that I am a Besht. Yesterday I started out from my home and I traveled swiftly on this long road. The fact is that after the death of her husband your daughter-in-law became a loose woman and slept with several Polish noblemen. In short, recently she promised an officer to change her religion and to marry him. Yesterday during the third meal, her grandfather, who was a famous tsaddik and a pillar of his generation, came to me from the upper world and asked me to correct his granddaughter, this woman, who has a lofty soul but who has fallen into demonic depths, so that she would not remain there, God forbid. I promised him. This woman planned that today, two hours from now, the officer would come with soldiers and take her by force together with all her clothing and jewelry, and she would change her religion. Therefore, I give this counsel. God will be with you and a great mitzvah will be credited to you for the saving of a soul."

The words penetrated to the heart of the householder and he believed him. The Besht promised him that he would return all the belongings that the woman took which were not hers. The Besht took the woman and brought her back with him. All the way back the Besht was kind to her, and she called him "my uncle."

Upon their arrival in the holy community of Medzhibozh the Besht arranged her engagement to a respectable, famous, and wealthy man. At the wedding, before the ceremony at the canopy, the woman came to the rabbi's room to confess and to ask repentance for her sins, since being in the rabbi's house had removed all the evil from her heart. When the Besht realized that she spoke from the depths of her heart, he said to her: "How could you imagine that I am your uncle? You should know that I am not your uncle. Because you fixed the time to convert, your grandfather asked me to save you, but if you do not make proper repentance you will die at once."

She wept great tears and asked him to tell her the way to repentance. The rabbi answered that this would be her repentance: "The marriage will be cancelled because you are not worthy of this man. After you experience the bitterness in your soul, you will marry a baker and sit in the market selling bagels. You will return all the belongings that your father-in-law gave you because it is not his crime and his sin. He gave them to you in his trust for me and in order to save your soul from hell."

She accepted the repentance wholeheartedly and became completely pious. After that her grandfather appeared in the Besht's dream and said to him: "You can rest now that you have eased my mind."[67]

What I am terming the "preamble" provides the first hint that something important is about to occur — the Besht is deep in thought. The matter is significant enough to prevent him from saying torah (giving his teaching) at the third meal, the most religiously crucial time of the week and the place where religious leadership is decided. The preamble suggests Besht's task is a secret; communicated to him from the Upper World — he does not say where he is going. His destination may in fact be unknown even to himself — the horses go by themselves, without human guidance. This would indicate to the audience an intimate connection between macrocosm and events in the microcosm. The horses' swift travel (qfizat ha derek) is important from the literary viewpoint, indicating both great distance, hence the significance of "place," and a sense of urgency.

The beginning of the tale presents an almost accidental encounter between the Besht and a half-dressed young woman. It is only later in the tale that the audience learns Besht knew the woman's history and identity. The Besht 'innocently' requests her to light his pipe. She does this without recognizing him, as a holy man, or perceiving that his pipe-smoking in fact constitutes a 'holy action.' Here the tale indicates the difference between the two distinct states of *devekuth*. *Katnuth*, the minor state, is preparation for *gadluth*, the major state. Smoking his pipe, the Besht is engaging in the *katnuth* phase of *devekuth*. Lighting the holy man's pipe is not merely incidental. The action makes contact between the *zaddik* and one who is in need of great help.[68]

---

[67]*In Praise*, pp. 245-47.

[68]Pipe-smoking may also be understood as performing a three-fold function: 1) elevating divine sparks, 2) driving away demons, and 3) 'relaxation' from the intensity of the *gadluth* stage of *devekuth*. Scholem

Her failure to recognize the holy man signifies the spiritual depths to which she has sunk; she appears before the holy man half-dressed. The *zaddik* mediates between upper and lower worlds by elevating those 'trapped' in the material. At this stage the Besht realizes that disclosing his true identity will prove fruitless. The *zaddik* can help only those willing to accept his assistance. Hence the Besht identifies himself as her uncle. He hopes that, as a 'family' member she will trust him, tell her story ('confess'), and change both her physical and spiritual place. The woman is portrayed as familialy isolated. She has a dead husband, a dead grandfather, a father-in-law, and a surrogate uncle. She lacks mother, father, sisters, or brothers. This serves to heighten her displaced situation.

The woman's tale is a miniature of the larger story; items are hidden, she mentions neither the Polish officer nor her intention to convert. Her words also require interpretive clarification. The existential despair she reveals is based apparently on her attachment to material things, but ultimately on her self-preoccupation. She is to be forced into marriage with her father-in-law's nephew. Her own husband has died, thereby depriving her of a source of clothes and jewelry, the most important things in the woman's life. The Besht suggests the first of two 'repentances' which appear in the tale. He offers her material well-being and integration into the family — I will be as a father to you . . . I will give you a good man as a husband. He appeals to her material and physical desires in order to persuade her to leave her place. These inducements are sufficient and the woman prepares to accompany the Besht to his town, and his home. Again, location is crucial. She has been 'reached' by the holy man on the level of the material. But the importance of her acceptance resides

---

is emphatic in stressing the two discrete phases of *devekuth*, and the type of activity which occurs in each. Gershom G. Scholem (ed.), *Devekuth,* or Communion with God," *The Messianic Idea in Judaism* (New York: Schocken, 1971), especially pp. 219-22.

Analysis of Specific Tales 45

in her attachment to the *zaddik,* even if, at this point, such attachment is for the 'wrong' reason. *Devekuth* also means clinging, or cleaving to, a group. Being in the presence of the *zaddik* or his community was tantamount to being in the presence of the divine. The woman gathers her clothes and jewels (her dowry) and prepares to leave with the Besht. This section concludes with the puzzlement of the householder at his daughter in-law's preparations for departure.

The middle of the tale encompasses two sections: the revelation and recognition of the Besht, and the woman's physical/spiritual change of place. The householder is angry at losing his property, and reacts out of a feeling of greed. Besht takes him into a closed room and reveals his true identity. At this time the audience learns why the Besht had been preoccupied during the third sabbath meal. He had received a visit from the woman's dead grandfather, a "famous tsaddik and a pillar of his generation," who was in the "upper world." This is a significant piece of information, for it indicates the importance with which the Besht is viewed up above. It also serves to emphasize the mediatorial role played by the Hasidic holy man. Besht further establishes his 'credentials' by declaring other secrets; the daughter-in-law has become a loose woman, she has promised to convert and marry a Polish officer. Nevertheless, the grandfather had stressed that the woman has a "lofty soul," *(neshamah g'vohah),* but had "fallen into demonic depths." She has, in other words, divine sparks in her soul, like every member of the community, but desperately needs assistance in elevating them. Unlike most possessors of secrets, the Besht does not have to "empirically verify" his words. The authority of the holy man is *sui generis.* The "performative" quality of his speech is evident.

The fact that Besht seeks out the woman illustrates the Hasidic notion that the *zaddik* must work among the people, i.e., descend from his elevated "rung."[69] The classical formulation of this theory is "descent in behalf of the ascent" *(yeridah zorekh aliyah)*, and the entire story may be seen as illustrative of this formula. The fact that the woman planned to convert and marry in only two hours underscores the sense of artistic 'emergency' as well as indicating that the *zaddik* saves sinners even at the last

---

[69]Scholem notes that The Besht was fond of the Talmudic anecdote of the two jesters. They do not sit at home thinking of their own salvation. Instead they work in the marketplace in order to make contact with the people at all levels. Scholem writes in detail: "Diese talmudische Anekdot, für die der Baalschem offenbar besonders viel übrig hatte und die in der Tat einen echt chassidischen Klang hat, erzählte davon, dass Rabbi Beroka den Marktplatz seiner Stadt in Babylonien aufzusuchen pflegte und der Prophet Elias ihn dort besuchte. Einmal fragte er ihn: Sind jetzt auf diesem Marktplatz irgend welche Kinder de kunftigen Welt (das heisst Anwärter auf die ewige Seligkeit)? Während er fragte, gingen zwei Brüder vorüber, und der Prophet Elias sagte: Diese beiden. Er ging und fragte sie: Was macht ihr? Sie sagten: Wir sind Possenreisser. Ist jemand traurig, se suchen wir ihn aufzuheitern, und sehen wir Leute streiten, so suchen wir Frieden zwischen ihnen zu stiften. Diese Spassmacher sind Gerechte nach dem Herzen des Baalschem. Sie sitzen nicht zu Haus und denken an ihr eigenes Heil. Sie arbeiten auf dem belebten und schmutzigen Marktplatz, wie er selbst zu tun liebte. Ihre Kraft zur Gottesgemeinschaft, wie er es sieht, bewährt sich in der Aufgabe, die Materie zu durchdringen und sie zum Geistigen zu erheben. Die unansehnliche Betätigung dient als Instrument der höchsten Leistung." Gershom G. Scholem, *Von der mystischen Gestalt der Gottheit* (Zurich: Rhein-Verlag, 1962), p. 123. It should be noted that *zaddikim* following the Besht tended to remain in place, i.e., their home, or "court." Hasidim would travel to the holy man. The sedentary *zaddik* symbolizes Hasidism's widespread acceptance. Weinryb, however, observes that the break with an itinerant *modus vivendi* was not complete, either for the Ba'al Shem Tov or the following *zaddikim*. Weinryb, *op. cit.*, p. 265.

moment. The householder is promised divine merit for helping to save a soul. He recognizes the Besht's true identity as a holy man and accepts the truth of what he has heard. On the pragmatic level, the householder is promised that he will receive back all goods taken by the daughter-in-law. The *zaddik* is portrayed as one who has the ability to put everything in its proper place.[70]

The middle portion of the tale concludes with the woman accompanying the Besht. He maintained contact with her, at her level, winning her trust and confidence — he was kind to her. Nevertheless, she was still "not in place," and thus unable to recognize the Besht — she called him "my uncle." This scene indicates movement, in both the literary and religious spheres. From a condition of religious exile, the woman is being brought home. The journey symbolizes the continuing elevation of the woman's soul, which is made possible by her attachment to the holy man.

The second recognition scene in the tale marks the woman's spiritual transformation. In order to repent, however, she must overcome attachment to material things. Hasidic doctrine claimed the material *qua* material, was not crucial. Its importance was in providing a vehicle for the proper worship of the divine. The woman's error, or sin, was in "stopping" with the material, and in failing to achieve either *kavvanah* or *devekuth*. To remedy this situation, the Besht arranged her marriage to a "respectable, famous, and wealthy man." Prior to the ceremony, however, the woman feels for the first time, the need genuinely to confess and truly to repent. The second confession is vastly different from the first. Previously, superficial and material considerations were important. Now, in the rabbi's house (a holy

---

[70]Scholem has drawn attention to the important fact that the mystic is called *zaddik,* or the Just man. "The just person in Jewish tradition is seen as the man who puts everything in its proper place and gives everything its due and thereby represents a social ideal of Judaism." *Mysticism and Society,*" p. 19.

place) all evil was removed from her heart.[71] She had moved from the lowest stage (the place of the householder) to a much higher stage (the house of the rabbi). Consequently she is now ready, and able, to recognize the true identity of the Besht, and to enter into a master-disciple relationship. The holy man tells her the truth; he is not her uncle. Her willingness to convert caused the intercession of both her grandfather (the upper world) and the Besht. She will die if her repentance is not proper. Since she is close to the upper world, anything less than full repentance would mean death. This does not, however, necessarily mean physical death. It suggests that if she misses this opportunity, she will descend back to the depths of sin, and no one will be able to help her elevate the sparks of her soul. She will be a victim of 'existential assassination.' In other words, exclusion from the community results in loss of socioreligious identity. But the woman had successfully undergone her initatory experience, and was now prepared for the final 'rite de passage.'

She will not marry the intended groom. As she is not "worthy," she would have been, again, out of place. Rather, she must 'interiorize' this self-knowledge — experience bitterness in her soul. Her marriage will instead be to a baker (a member of the right class). Her task will be to sit in the market selling bagels. Her rightful place is to be in corporeality, but with the significant difference that now she will use this time as an opportunity for worship *('avodah be-gashmiyyut),* concentrating on *devekuth.*

---

[71]The Hebrew text uses the passive *(na'aqor)* of the verb "to remove" *(la'aqor).* Samuel A. Horodezky, ed., *Sefer Shivhei ha Besht* (Tel Aviv: Dvir, 1968), p. 163. This indicates the importance of place, i.e., the rabbi's house, as well as presence — the holy man — in the repentance process. In the Lurianic system, *shevirath ha-kelim* (breaking of the vessels) symbolized the significance of place on a cosmic level, i.e., "A being not in its place is in exile. Thus since that primordial act, all being has been a being in exile, in need of being led back and redeemed." Gershom G. Scholem, *On the Kabbalah and Its Symbolism,* trans. by R. Manheim (New York: Schocken Books, 1969), p. 112.

The last connection with her former existence is to be severed. She must return her father-in-law's belongings. He had only given them because he trusted the Besht, and he wanted to save his daughter-in-law's soul from hell. Clinging to the holy man (being in the right place) obviates any need for harmful secondary activity such as cleaving to one's material possessions, or preoccupation with self.

By this time the story has suggested three choices concerning marriage. Each choice has implications for the community, but only one of them results in harmony. The father-in-law wished the girl to marry his nephew, thereby keeping control of his property (the dowry). His motive was greed. The woman herself was similarly motivated — she planned to take all the clothing and jewelry. Her conversion would place her beyond the safety of the community. Not only would she have been out of place, she would have seriously impaired her chances for salvation. The Besht's solution restored the woman, religiously and physically. The further the woman progressed in the master-disciple relationship, the lower her social status became until, finally, after experiencing total contrition, she became completely righteous. Her reintegration into the holy man's 'community' means that she is in place. Engaging in honest labor with the proper intention, experiencing self-understanding, and recognizing the efficacy of one's community and the holy man are indications, for Hasidism, of normalized religious experience. The story disapproves, implicitly, of the unmarried state. As superficial as her reasons were, the woman recognized the necessity of marriage. Being single, then, emerges as one more example of being out of place.[72]

---

[72]The unity represented by marriage was thought to imitate, and stimulate on the microcosmic level, the unity of God and the Shekhinah, on the macrocosmic level. The Besht had anticipated ascending to heaven like Elijah. But the death of his wife prevented this from happening. He comments: "I expected to ascend in a storm, but now that I am only part of a body it is impossible, and I am grieved." Tale 146, "Ascension to Heaven," *In Praise,* p. 169.

The goal of the story is to portray the holy man performing one of his most important duties, calling to repentance a community member who is on the verge of conversion.[73] Existence in the sphere of the material without proper *devekuth* is dangerous. Escaping the confines of the material means avoiding the snares of *kelipoth*. The audience hearing the tale can learn several important things. The *zaddik* is always willing to help them, no matter how low they have descended. Disguises served to underscore the fact that one could never know who might be a holy man. The elaborate kinship structure served to emphasize the communal nature of normalization.[74] Community determines identity and salvation; *extra ecclesiam nulla salus*.

A variant of "The Loose Woman," tale 138, "The Adulteress," portrays the danger implicit in the unmarried state. A woman, abandoned by her husband, has intercourse with her gentile servant. Her brothers, fearful that she will abandon Judaism, conspire to kill her. The existential assassination is here followed by a planned physical assassination. The Besht intervenes, by means of swift travel, and saves her life. She became a "thoroughly repentant sinner." The woman could frequently be found standing in the mikveh (ritual bath) at midnight. *In Praise,* pp. 163-64.

[73]Judaism takes a dim view of conversion. It is one of the gravest sins, and the convert is often considered "dead."

[74]The Besht is reported as having observed that every Jew is a member of the *Shekhinah* (community of Israel). But, referring to the apostacy of the Frankists (eighteenth century Jewish heretics), "when the member is cut off there is no possible repair." *In Praise,* p. 59.

Analysis of Specific Tales

Tale number 32, "The Melamed's Dream," illustrates the extreme importance with which early Hasidism viewed dreams. Dreams functioned in various capacities: as media of instruction, aids in conversion, and prophetically. Peter Berger observes that dreams and nocturnal visions can be related to daily existence in a variety of ways as 1) warnings, 2) prophecies, 3) decisive encounters with the sacred, and 4) having specific consequences for everyday conduct in society.[75] Moreover, realities represented in dreams, or as Berger terms them, marginal situations, are given higher cognitive status than everyday reality.

In the Holy Community of Medzhibozh there was a rich man who was not in sympathy with the Besht, and he employed a melamed (tutor) for his children, a very learned man, knowledgeable in every way, who also kept away from the Besht. And the (Besht) wanted very much to attract him to the worship of God, since good fortune was waiting for him. But the Besht wondered how it would come about as the melamed kept far away, especially since his employer watched him very carefully.

Once on a Friday night, the melamed dreamed that he was strolling all over the holy community of Medzhibozh, and he saw a wonderful palace, which was elaborately decorated in every conceivable way. The more he looked the more wonderful things he saw. And when he took pains to concentrate on the beauty of the craftsmanship, he was astonished because every minute space contained wisdom and skill as had never before been seen in the whole world. His heart perceived the great wisdom, and he was attracted to it with all his soul.

When he approached the window to look inside, behold, he saw the Besht and his entire holy group seated around the table, and the Besht was saying torah. He was filled with excitement and he

---

[75]Peter Berger, *The Sacred Canopy* (New York: Doubleday & Company, Inc., 1967), p. 43.

The Melamed's Dream Place

Copyright © 1977 Ellen Steinfeld

wanted to reach the innermost section of the building. He ran toward the door, but . . . the attendant pushed him aside and did not let him enter. He felt deeply grieved. Nevertheless, in spite of all this, his strong desire to listen to the living words of God was so great that he stood at the window and heard all the Besht's holy words.

He woke up and it was a dream. He began to repeat the torah that he heard and it was sweeter than honey. He repeated it twice and three times, but since it was only midnight he fell asleep again.

In the morning when he got up . . ., he realized that he still remembered the dream very clearly, but the torah had slipped from his mind altogether. He grieved about the loss until he was so beset with despair that he did not know how he managed to pray. At breakfast he sat bewildered.

Perhaps he would have gone to the Besht by himself, but he recalled that in the dream the servant rebuffed him, and he was afraid that it would be so in reality as well and that he would endure disgrace and shame. And he grieved greatly all day.

At the third meal the Besht ordered: "Go to the house of that wealthy man and tell the melamed to come here." They were greatly amazed by it.

When the messenger opened the door and said to the melamed, "The Besht invites you, sir, to come to him," he immediately leaped over the table and ran without his overcoat like a madman. Then he heard all the torah that he had heard at night, and he immediately fainted.

When he caught his breath again the Besht said to him jokingly: "If you had heard new things, you would have reason to be so excited, but this is not new since you heard all this last night." And he understood that what had happened was from God, and he followed the Besht wholeheartedly and he became a truly righteous man.[76]

The preamble provides a glimpse of the social friction which existed between the wealthy and the incipient Hasidic movement. Eastern European Jewry was rigidly stratified; the rich were, *de facto,* in positions of considerable influence concerning *kehilla* matters, including leadership. The relationship between the *melamed* who, while remaining nameless is described as a great scholar, and Hasidism is ambiguous. On the one hand, he is portrayed as keeping away from the Besht. This would indicate that the *melamed* himself had no interest in Hasidism. On the other hand, we are told that the *melamed* kept his distance, at least in part, because of an external factor — "his employer watched him very carefully." From the literary viewpoint, it is possible to observe an implicit dichotomy: Learning versus "true," i.e., Hasidic, piety. The *melamed's* scholarly knowledge of Judaism is insufficient for genuine salvation.

Besht is perplexed. He does not know how to attract the *melamed* "to the worship of God," i.e., the Hasidic mode of worship which stressed enthusiastic and demonstrative piety. Good fortune — salvation — awaited the *melamed*. The seriousness of the matter is hinted at by the fact that the Besht himself was unsure how the *melamed* was to be attracted. Besht "wondered how it would come about . . . ." The preamble has, from a literary point of view, established an expectation that the Besht will receive assistance from the upper worlds in order to solve this vexing problem. The *zaddik's* cosmic powers will be employed in an attempt at overcoming an obstacle in the social realm. Moreover, the reader is reminded that events in the microcosm have reverberations in the macrocosm. No activity "below" escapes notice of those "above."

The first section of the tale relates the contents of the *melamed's* dream. In his dream, he leaves the watchful eye of his employer while "strolling all over the holy community of Medzhibozh" (the center of Beshtian Hasidism). The *melamed,* not unlike the

---

[76] *In Praise,* pp. 46-48.

"Loose Woman," is in the wrong place — if not physically, at least spiritually. Initially, the *melamed's* path toward salvation requires him to leave the direct influence and control of the rich. The scholar is portrayed as *experiencing* an overwhelming desire to look at a particular structure.

It is significant to note that while the usual characterizations of Beshtian Hasidism stress, correctly, its emphasis upon nontheoretical devices in attracting followers, the *melamed* is fascinated, in his dream, by an "elaborately decorated" edifice which required "pains" (cerebral effort) to concentrate upon. But the "palace" is merely *attractive* on the superficial level. Its real significance lies in penetrating its depths. One must move from the periphery to the center.

The "palace" is, clearly, no ordinary structure — "every minute space contained wisdom and skill as had never before been seen in the whole world." Moreover, the *melamed* perceived its wisdom not *intellectually*, but with his *"heart."* This represents a significant departure from the type of cognition which served to distinguish *melamdim* from Hasidim. In my opinion, the importance of this section resides in the *melamed's* observation that "since the outside of the palace was so ornate the inside would be even more so." This statement can be taken as a metaphor describing the *melamed's* own condition. As a trained halakhic scholar, the *melamed* represents the "palace." His knowledge, however, was confined to the cerebral mode. Failing to interiorize his learning, he remains outside the true intention of Judaism, at least according to the Hasidic interpretation of the tradition. Stated in terms of Hasidic praxis the *melamed* has failed to achieve the correct *kavvanah* in his studies. Instead of serving as a vehicle of worship and a means of bringing him close to God, the *melamed's* intellectual efforts have hampered his attempts to achieve *devekuth*. The *melamed* has not been able to transform his study into a salvific ritual.

Desiring to look inside, the *melamed* sees the Besht and his disciples seated around a table, where the Besht "was saying torah." This "filled" the *melamed* with excitement. The Besht's "torah" — mystical exegesis — is an interpretation by one who is allegedly inferior, at least concerning the subtleties of halakhic Judaism, to the *melamed,* a highly trained scholar. The reader, or listener, is implicitly reminded at this time that study or erudition for its own sake *(lishmah),* and lacking *kavvanah* is a religiously deficient activity.[77] Besht, as a *zaddik* is, on the other hand, able to provide answers to even the most difficult halakhic problems. His prowess derives from his contact with the upper worlds. Moreover, the Besht's knowledge is, unlike that of the *melamed,* never viewed as an end in itself. Rather, his interpretive skills are always employed in order to demonstrate the superiority of Hasidic piety.

The *melamed* is excited by the Besht's teachings. Removed from the restrictive influence of the rich and the superficial, the scholar begins to experience a desire to respond positively to the Hasidic message. Despite his erudition and his evident change of heart, the *melamed* is not yet worthy of being physically close to the *zaddik.* An attendant bars the *melamed* from entering the door. The scholar must pass through an initiatory scenario, during which process he will attain insight into the severe limitations of his present type of existence, and the superiority of the *zaddikim.* His deep grief at being prevented from joining the Hasidim constitutes the first step on the *melamed's* salvific path. Despite his grief, which may be understood as the incipient stage

---

[77]Tale 173 reports that the Besht "scolded" a great scholar, saying: "Is it to argue and tease that we learn the Torah?" Upon hearing the *zaddik's* words, the scholar sees his error and "converts" to Hasidism. *In Praise,* p. 189. Rabbi Ya'akov Yosef Ha-Cohen, author of *Toledot Ya'akov Yosef,* the first Hasidic book, was similarly disuaded from pursuing a barren scholarly approach to Judaism. At first a severe critic of Hasidism, Ya'akov Yosef is converted to Hasidic ways by the Besht himself, who points out the futility of scholarship which is practiced without the purpose of coming closer to God.

Analysis of Specific Tales

of recognition, the *melamed's* desire to hear Besht's torah, i.e., "the living words of God," compelled him to stand at the window, listening to the Besht's "holy words."[78]

The first section concludes with the *melamed* awakening from his dream. Repeating the torah which he had heard, three times, he found it "sweeter than honey." This tale, like that of the "Loose Woman," suggests that the *zaddik* is able to attract each one at their own level. Unlike the Loose Woman, however, the *melamed* requires no assurance of material well-being in order to follow the Besht. The *melamed* is attracted to the Besht by a patently cerebral device. Moreover, the *melamed's* spiritual condition is evidently superior to the woman's, i.e., it was unnecessary for the Besht to disguise himself before the scholar. The *melamed's* dream is, in fact, a first "call" to repentance, and indicates the extraordinary prominence which Hasidism attached to information revealed in dreams.[79]

The tale's second section contains a crucial recognition scene. Upon waking, in the morning, the *melamed* discovered that he distinctly remembered the dream, but failed to recall the Besht's torah. This failure indicates that the scholar has not yet overcome the limitations of his old, i.e., rabbinic, plausibility structure. However, the *melamed* "grieved" over his inability to recall the Besht's teachings to such an extent that it was difficult for him to say the morning prayer in the "old," rabbinic manner, and he could not eat his breakfast. The attempts of his wealthy employer to console him are fruitless. The old "remedies" no longer are effective. This second experience of grief differs from the first one in intensity as well as in final outcome. The *melamed's* grief, this

---

[78]The voice of the *shekhinah* was believed to speak from the *zaddik's* throat.

[79]The Besht is alleged to have discovered the "Hasidic way" of worship during a dream. *Fun Rebin's Hauf*, pp. 91-94, cited by Newman, *op. cit.*, p. 412.

time, leads to his recognition that his present plausibility structure is incomplete. He realizes that his eruditon and scholarship are merely empty forms. His religious practice lacked proper devotion and real enthusiasm.

Although the *melamed* wanted to join the Besht, he feared that because he had been denied this opportunity in his dream, he would be refused admittance. If this were to happen, the *melamed* was certain that he would "endure disgrace and shame." Consequently he "grieved greatly" throughout the day (Saturday). The observation concerning "disgrace and shame" is important. It reveals the fact that the *melamed* still is not ready to make the "existential commitment" required of him as a follower of the Besht. Instead, the scholar betrays a certain weakness of character — he worries about shame and disgrace, external problems — rather than risking existence itself in order to achieve completeness, i.e., become a hasid. Further transformation is required. This, in my opinion, is the intention of the scholar's daylong grief, which can be understood as including abstinence from food and drink. It is a literary device implying continuation of the initiatory process begun with the onset of his dream. Moreover, the grief may also be viewed as penance for having ignored or doubted the (mystical) wisdom of the *zaddikim*. Finally, his initiatory experience prepares the *melamed* for acceptance by the Hasidic community.

The third section is introduced by a scene from the *se'udah shelishith,* an explicitly mystical occasion among the Hasidim. Besht dispatches a messenger to fetch the *melamed.* The disciples, his Hasidim, are unaware of the *melamed's rite de passage.* Consequently, they are "greatly amazed" by the Besht's actions. Besht's "invitation" to the *melamed* is another example of the *zaddik* performing his most important function, the call to repentance — which implies elevating one's efforts in the world. Upon receiving the Besht's summons, the *melamed* "leaped over the table and ran without his overcoat like a madman." This ecstatic outburst is significant. It suggests that among Beshtian

Hasidim the expectation is that inner experience will transform behavior.

The *melamed's* encounter with the Besht reveals important information about the *zaddik's* cosmic role. He has the ability not only to interpret men's dreams, but to know the contents of these dreams prior to being told. The Besht is assited in his task by those in the "upper world." He orders the *melamed* brought to him at the third meal. Prior to this time, the Besht himself was portrayed as uncertain how to proceed in the case of the *melamed*. In his mystical capacity, the Besht serves as a vital link between macrocosm and microcosm. His "marvelous knowledge" is a device which is employed in the task of helping individuals recognize the connection between events in the microcosm and actions in the macrocosm.

The tale concludes with the *melamed's* recognition that what had occurred "was from God." Renouncing his old ways, the *melamed* becomes a "truly righteous man" and a genuine follower of the Besht.

There is a clear and distinct pattern of movement in the tale. The *melamed's* life is essentially superficial and thus open to change. He is portrayed, initially, as indifferent or hostile to Hasidism. The *melamed's rite de passage* from outsiderhood to communal member occurs in stages. At first he is attracted by a *visual* experience of the palace. There follows an *auditory* experience of the Besht's torah. Underlying these experiences is the "call" to a new type of existence. Growing in intensity, the call results in the *melamed's* recognition of the futility of rabbinism and the sterility of the wealthy. The *melamed* becomes an adherent of enthusiastic religiosity. His upward integration into the Hasidic community reveals a struggle between two competing types of piety; the scholarly restrained approach to religion is abandoned in favor of emotional self-expression. Broadly speaking, a rabbinic plausibility structure was replaced by a mysticopietistic plausibility structure. The *melamed*, like the Loose Woman, had finally to overcome excessive preoccupation with the self. Although an observant Jew, unlike the Loose Woman, the *melamed's* life was as incomplete as the woman's. Both, on different levels, had to be awakened to the possibilities of *devekuth* and the need for *kavvanah* whether on a cerebral or a noncerebral level.

Conclusion

To view Beshtian Hasidism as a normalized or inner-worldly type of mysticism provides better means of treating the range of data pertinent to the study of mysticism. This is not to claim that Hasidic mysticism itself was all of one piece. A definite current of elitism — world-fleeing contemplation — emerged after the third generation. The so-called *dissident* nineteenth-century Hasidism of Przysucha and Kotzk, for example, emphasized the cosmic at the expense of the social elements of mysticism. Moreover, as a "living" religious movement Hasidic mysticism is capable of producing a variety of new modes of mystical expression. Nevertheless, for Beshtian Hasidism cosmic themes are portrayed in a clearly social setting. Normalization does not imply a lack of specificity, nor is it antimonian. Nor, for that matter, does it imply that every communal member is a mystic. Normalization means that even social roles have cosmic implications, and that all individuals may participate in the salvific enterprise. The *zaddik* in his cosmic task mediates between the divine and the human worlds. The holy man leads a holy community comprised of those professing allegiance to the *zaddik*.

In the tales which I have analyzed, the mystic's task was seen to consist primarily of assisting individuals in elevating their personal sparks. These sparks reside everywhere. Consequently, all that one does is potentially salvific, if performed with the correct intention. The *zaddik's* teaching takes many forms: conversation, discourse, dream manipulation, tales, and even physical gestures and facial expression. All are efficacious. Normalized mysticism suggests that each one, according to his level, is able to participate in the salvific quest. The "Loose Woman" implied that fear of chaos caused by scattered divine sparks and resultant disruption of primal unity, changes to fear of conversion, of Christians, and of demons, all interfere with one's salvation by being in the wrong place. The "Melamed's Dream," on its part, demonstrated that even a central Jewish category such as learning is incomplete unless accompanied by the correct ritual attitude. "Learning" can occur on many levels. The important point is that no level is excluded. Stress is on "simple" activities, e.g., the telling of tales and the importance of the experiential dimension. Normalization suggests that both mystic and community are transformed. Normalized mysticism possesses an alchemical dimension. Its purpose is to transform one's perception of the apparently "ordinary," by constantly reminding those concerned of the intimate relationship which exists between microcosmic and macrocosmic events. This transformation makes mysticism an inclusive religious category, legitimately concerned with communal and sociological phenomena.